IN JESUS' NAME

In Jesus' Name

JUDITH HEANEY

Copyright © 2024 by Judith Heaney and Out of the Boat Books
Cover art by Brigid McKee
All rights reserved. No part of this book may be reproduced in any manner whatsoever without written permission except in the case of brief quotations embodied in critical articles and reviews.
First Printing, 2024
www.judithheaney.com

PREFACE

The prayers in this book come from my personal prayer journey and reflect a small part of my morning and evening times in the presence of God. They in no way indicate anything more than an attempt to draw near to the heart of God, and I hope they provide that opportunity for you, dear reader, as well. May they inspire you and encourage you in your daily prayers.

May they be a guide for you. May you remember this is your prayer journey, and prayers are meant as a conversation you get to have with the One who not only created the universe but who designed you. He wants to know you and He wants you to know Him. And no words are off limits. Truly. God is big enough for our pain as well as our praise and for our lament as well as our laughter. He is big enough to handle our anger and anxiety alongside our wonder and worship.

As you spend time with God, I pray you will experience His presence in new ways. I pray He will reveal Himself to You in unique and specific ways you will come to recognize and understand deep in your heart.

One final note—you will discover I have chosen to capitalize references to God (He, Him, Lord, King, etc). This is a personal choice and my way of acknowledging the majesty of God and who He is as Creator. I have also chosen to capitalize the word *Truth* in many places; those instances, for me, represent the absolute Truth of God and His Word.

Judith Heaney
Asheville
December, 2024

~ Day 1 ~

PERSEVERANCE...

Good and gracious God, King of the universe, I come into Your presence to seek Your face and draw near to You and ask You as the God of our refuge and strength to provide me the strength necessary to persevere through these current circumstances and challenges. I confess, Lord, I am overwhelmed but earnestly seeking Your strength and Your help and Your guidance right now. I hate how I feel and how I am responding to the people in my life as a result of the stress of life's circumstances. There are no easy answers and I am angry as well as overwhelmed. God, help me, please. Provide me the grace and the strength to move forward and to move through today.

Show me the way I should go. Help me, Lord, to follow You because, honestly, I don't know where we are supposed to be going right now. Sometimes I don't have strength to persevere, God. I just don't. I want to ask "Why,"; but I won't. Instead I will ask "What?" – What do You want me to do God? What is the focus supposed to be right now? What are You doing in these circumstances, Lord?

Take the bitterness and anger and resentment from me. Take the fear and the doubts and the worries and concerns from me. Provide me clarity and wisdom for the next step, today's next steps, one step at a time.

I have no other words to pray right now because I do not have peace or strength today. Instead I have a deep sadness and overwhelm and can't hear You or any answers You may or may not be providing right now. Even so, I trust You with what little ability and strength I have and ask You to help me overcome my unbelief.

And I ask all of this in Jesus' name, Amen.

~ Day 2 ~

PRAYER, PETITION & THANKSGIVING

Good morning, good and gracious and loving God. Thank You for the gift of this new day and for Your presence here with me this morning. I am grateful I have the invitation and opportunity to enter this time and place with You, to sit in Your presence and to remember who You are and to remember Your faithfulness and to recall Your promises. As I sit with You, I want to surrender this day and my life to You because I want to have Your version of the day ahead and not mine. I know and acknowledge Your perfect plan and will and I confess my desire to embrace those in my life and my day today. May Your will be done, God, not mine.

Lord God, I desperately need You. I am tired of my cares and concerns and anxieties taking center stage in my life each and every day. So today I am coming to You with my prayers, petitions, and thanksgiving. I want to give You my focus and attention. I want to surrender control to You and to admit You know better than I do what this day needs to include and look like. Lead me. Guide me. Place my feet on the right path for Your Name's sake. Let there be moments today where I lie down in green pastures and rest beside calm waters. Restore my soul and speak to my heart so it is aligned with Yours.

Let there be moments of praise and worship and glorifying You. Let there be moments of seeing You at work in me and in my life. Let me honor You in my choices and let my life be a reflection of You, a reflection of hope and joy and strength from You and in You.

Thank You, God, for this beautiful day with its cooler feel and gentle breeze rustling leaves in the trees outside the window. For the sunshine and the sense of seasons shifting and new things on the shifting horizon. Thank You, Lord, for a sense of anticipation and for a sense of You being near. Let my eyes and my heart see You working in me and in my circumstances today, and let me not forget to pause and praise You because of who You are and what You are doing in me and for me.

Help me today to love You more, to know You more, and to live out my life for You.

I ask these things in Jesus' name, Amen.

~ Day 3 ~

YOU ARE MY PORTION

Good and gracious God, You are my portion, my provision, and my hope. I place my hope in You because You are faithful and unchanging and You care for me. You are intimately involved in even the smallest details of my life here in this world. Because of that, I know without a doubt I am not alone. Not even now when my broken soundtracks amplify and tell me lies about my circumstances, I know You care not only about my circumstances, but You care about me and my family. You are a God who is invested in me as well as in the moments of and the people in my life.

I give You thanks for this. I give you thanks that I am alive and safe and I am not alone. And

I cry out to You in gratitude but also, at least in part, Lord, in lament. There is so much division and heartache and uncertainty in this world, but You are my portion. You are my refuge. You are my certainty. Indeed, You are my strength, God. Right now, like Moses, I hide myself in the crevice of the rock, knowing You are here and Your hand is upon me. You provide me a glimpse of You and let me live even though I know no one can see Your face and live. I am here on holy ground and I bend low before you, acknowledging You as my life and my every breath.

Lord, I draw my strength from You. I trust You and wait on You to meet me here and guide me with Your wisdom. I feel You take my hand in Your right hand as You lead me along the ancient paths and I know I am okay. I am more than okay. Crack wide open my heart and my mind and pour out Your wisdom and Your goodness until my heart and mind overflow with them. Crack wide my heart and mind and drip the fire of Your Holy Spirit into me so I am refined in the fire of His purifying presence and renewed in hope and peace and love and joy. Touch my life with the flaming coal and purify my lips. Renew in me a clean heart and lead me along righteous paths for Your sake, gracious God, and renew in me a sense of passion and purpose as we continue to move forward into the day ahead together.

Today I will breathe in and out, remembering that my every breath comes from You. I will give You thanks and praise Your name in each moment, finding things for which I am grateful. Make a way today, Lord, and go out before me into the day and my circumstances and the world and guide me according to Your incredible goodness.

I pray these things in Jesus' name.

~ Day 4 ~

PEACE & ABUNDANCE

Oh dear Heavenly Father, how grateful am I this morning to sit here with You and raise up my thanksgiving and praise. How I want to acknowledge You and Your goodness this morning; I want to acknowledge Your provision, Your protection, Your peace and Your abundance. Thank You for who You are and for Your presence here with me, Your child. Thank You for the gift of Your Holy Spirit, my Counselor and Advocate and Teacher, who reminds me of who You are and calls to mind the Truth I find in Your Word.

Thank You, God, that storms have passed; they are now done and moved on and I am safe here with You. Thank You for the protection

You provided me. Be a comfort, and pour out Your peace and no-matter-what love on each and every person who is waking up in the aftermath of whatever storms they have faced, whether natural disasters or with friends or family, or even within themselves. Meet each person where they are and be their strength and their protection. Be their peace and abundance this morning as only You can (add the names of those for whom you wish to pray specifically).

God, as I look out at today, I invite You to join me in my day and to help plan out my tasks and my work. Give me Your perspective and help me to see the world as You desire it and created it to be. Help me to be Your image bearer today in all I do and say.

This morning, Father, I raise up to Your care family and friends and ask You to meet each of them where they are starting their day today. Be their hope and their joy and be their peace and their abundance. Pour out Your love and grace and guide them in Your wisdom. I pray for these people to whom I am connected and for whom I care (include names of those for whom you would like to pray). Be a refuge and be their peace and abundance as they move through the day ahead. Thank You, God, for Your goodness and love.

I pray all these things in Jesus' name, Amen.

~ Day 5 ~

YOU CONQUERED THE WORLD

Dear Heavenly Father, how great You are. How mighty to save. How just and faithful and righteous. You are holy and yet You invite us into Your presence to speak with You and to cast our cares and concerns on You. You are ready to meet with us and to listen to us and to pour out Your peace that passes all understanding over us. You invite us to know You and to be known by You. Please, God, forgive me for the times I take You and Your invitation for granted or for when I have sidestepped Your invitation in an effort to do life on my own terms and in my own way. Thank You for grace and mercy and do-overs. Thank You for Your promises and Your faithfulness.

Thank You for conquering the world and for being a God who is intimately interested in and familiar with me and my life and whatever things concern me. Thank You for hearing my heart and listening to my prayers and for inviting me to use You as my refuge, reminding me that there will be troubles in this world but You are with me in the face of all of them and You have overcome this world with its challenges and struggles, as well as its evil and death. You have defeated the evil one and I can rest in You always, no matter what.

It is time for me today to exercise my creative muscles and to do creative work alongside You. You invite me to work with You, to create with You. You place my feet upon the right paths for Your sake. Help me to follow You on that path today. Help me to see and live for eternity and provide me Your eternal perspective. Remind me that all I do contributes to my eternal hope and my journey toward You and heaven, always toward eternity. May the choices I make and the words I speak reflect You to this weary and desperate world and even more to my friends and family, who need to see You for Who You are and the mercy and life You offer.

I pray these things in Jesus' name, Amen.

~ Day 6 ~

LET YOUR WORDS REMAIN IN ME

Oh good and gracious God, thank You for this day. Thank You for the sun that is shining and for the birds that are singing and for the colors of Your creation that stir my soul and remind me who You are in all Your creative power. Thank You for designing and creating me with the same care and love with which You designed the details of the universe.

Lord, as I move through my day today, let me live out the words from John 15:7: "If you remain in me and my words remain in you, ask whatever you want and it will be done for you." Let Your words remain in me; by Your Holy Spirit help me remain in You and help Your words remain in me so that I am influenced and guided by Your never-changing Truth. I understand the second part of the verse must be informed and guided by the first part — wherein I remain in You and am infused with Your eternal Truth and perspective and guided in my wants and needs and prayer requests by Your words that are in me, that are a part of me. Only then are my desires aligned with Yours and my heart aligned with Yours. It is only when my desires have been brought into alignment with Yours that I will ask you for my heart's desires. Until then, I ask you to make my heart's desires Your desires. Remove the chaff of my selfishness and self-centeredness and bring about the refining change that my heart both desires and needs today.

Thank You for this gift of You and Your presence and the opportunities Your gift brings with it—a peace that passes all understanding and the opportunity to intercede for others, to carry their burdens in prayer before Your throne of grace (take a moment to pray for those in your life, for friends, family, colleagues, and strangers).

God, be with me along the path I travel today and use the nudging of Your Holy Spirit to help me keep my focus on You in the tasks set before me, whether mundane, ordinary, creative, or important. Remind me all tasks are important to You and each can be an act of worship when done for You and Your glory. Let my response to You and to my works today be one of obedience and faithfulness, trusting You with the outcomes both in my life and in my heart and soul and spirit as You use the work of my hands to refine me and to build Your kingdom. Remind me how much You care for me and let my attitude and response reflect this Truth. Let Your love shine through me into the lives of others and those with whom I cross paths today, whether in person or online.

I pray all these things this morning in Jesus' name, Amen.

~ Day 7 ~

YOUR WORDS ARE PURE WORDS

Oh Lord, my good and gracious Heavenly Father, thank You for who You are and for Your words that greet me every morning when I open my Bible or reading the Daily Refresh on my Bible app or open my journal of prayer and focus on You. Your words are pure and Your words are true. Let Your words fill me this morning. Let Your words inform me and guide me along the right and ancient paths for Your Name's sake. Lord, today, let me release hold of the undercurrent of any anger or doubt or worry in my life and let me experience You and Your joy fully and deeply and without holding back. Help me to live out the visions I hold in my mind of the life I see and the ways I want to be in the world and with my family and in the work You have provided me to do.

Lord, infuse me with Your grace and mercy and allow me to delight in You in child-like wonder. Help me today to trust You more than yesterday and to take You at Your Word because Your words are pure words. Reveal to me what this means and what it looks like as I move through this morning and into my day.

Right now I give You my thanks and my praise and pray these things in Jesus' name, Amen.

~ Day 8 ~

HOPE + JOY = PEACE

Good and gracious God in heaven, I come into Your presence and acknowledge You as the King of kings and the Lord of lords, as the rightful and true King who is indeed King of the universe. My mind buzzes and pulses with thoughts, many that are not even fully formed or fully coherent to me, but I know You see me and You know those thoughts as well as You know my heart and my concerns. Thank You, God, that You invite me here this morning to soak in Your mercy and to absorb Your grace. You are a God of hope and for that I am deeply grateful because sometimes I step out and into the day without letting You restore my hope or my joy or without inviting You to be a part of each and every moment; therefore I move through my day without the peace You offer and that passes all understanding.

As part of my prayer this morning, Lord, I speak the words from Romans 15:13—Now may the God of hope fill you with all joy and peace as you believe so that you may overflow with hope by the power of the Holy Spirit.

What wonderful words these are, words whose power renews my weary soul and inspires my faith this morning. These words inspire my faith to persevere and to hold fast to the Truth I know about You.

Thank You, God, for the beauty You created in this world, for the bird songs that are sweet and varied and that raise up like praise and thanksgiving this morning.

Thank You, God, for blue skies and lush landscapes that remind me how You provide water for the earth and sun so plants can grow, just as You provide what I need each day.

Thank You, God, for night skies filled with stars and meteors (even if I was unable to see them as I so desired), each testifying to the power and creativity of Your Creation.

Thank You, God, for a no-matter-what kind of love that encourages and demands the same from me even though we both know I will fall short of Your example in Christ who laid down His life for mine.

Thank You, God, for Your ever-present presence and Your still small voice and the words of the prophets who reveal Your character through the Bible.

Thank You, God, for Your mercy and grace that renew my faith and wipe the slate clean for this brand new day.

Thank You, God, for the good works prepared so long ago for me to step into. Help me to walk in Your ways and step into those good works today as Your Spirit leads me and guides me in thought, word, and deed.

Help me to pray for others today no matter who they are or how differently we see the world.

Soften my heart, God, and open my eyes to see the world from Your eternal perspective.

Your ways are not my ways and Your thoughts are not my thoughts, but You have the power to refine my faith, my ways, and my thoughts, and I give You permission to do that today by surrendering my heart and my life and my desires and my plans to You. Align my heart with Yours and give me the desires of my heart according to Your goodness as You align my desires with Yours.

I pray all these things in Jesus' name, Amen.

~ Day 9 ~

MY HELP IS YOU

Good and gracious God, King of the universe, thank You for this brand new day and all it holds. Thank You for waking me up this morning and for providing me with Yourself and with the leading of Your Holy Spirit. I am grateful I can call out to You as I start my day and You hear my prayers. You know my needs and You have plans for me I cannot truly envision or even imagine. Thank You.

As I step into today, be with me and lead me along the right paths You have planned for me to follow today for Your Name's sake. My help is in You for all the things I will do or face today. This day stretches before me with possibility and opportunities and I want to honor You in all I do. Help me to be productive today and to complete the tasks set before me. Open my eyes to the good works You designed for me to step into so long ago.

Today is a long day, filled with things I want to do and need to do. Be with me and direct my steps. I surrender all of me to all of You. I acknowledge You as the One who has the best for me, far better than anything I can create or plan for myself. My help is You. My life is in Your hands, and, truly, I want to live for You every moment of today. Go out before me and help me to sense the nudging of Your Holy Spirit as He guides me in my choices and decisions. Ignite my creativity and pour out Your desires for me and fill my heart with them. Let my heart truly reflect You in all my ways today.

In Jesus' name I pray these things, Amen.

~ Day 10 ~

THE HOLY GROUND OF PRAYER

Good morning good and gracious God, King of the Universe and Lord of lords. Thank You for this beautiful new day with all its sights and sounds that remind me of Your creativity and inspire wonder within me. There are colors all around, and the sun burns brightly behind gray clouds to remind me even when I cannot see it and there is no bright blue sky above, still the sun is there, alighting the clouds with its glow and pouring out from above. In moments like these I am reminded of You—that even when I cannot see You at work around me or even within me, or when I cannot sense Your presence in my circumstances,

You are with me. You are faithful and I can trust You and Your words because You are who You say You are. I can see You and Your character in the life and actions of Jesus as told in the Gospels. Thank You, God, for inspiring the disciples and other writers of the New Testament and Old Testament books to share their testimonies and revelations from Your Holy Spirit so we have a record of Jesus and accounts of Your ways to guide us in our lives today. May I cling to those Truths always as I live out the days of my life.

Lord, I am filled with wonder as I consider who You are. I am equally overflowing with thanksgiving because of Your ever-present presence with me. I take comfort in knowing You are with me, guiding me by Your Holy Spirit who dwells in me and pours out wisdom whenever I request it. And I am thankful for Your Word and the reminder in the scriptures to seek Your wisdom often and to lean on You and Your understanding rather than on my own. I am grateful I do not have to navigate this world or my circumstances in my limited power or abilities.

As I sit before Your throne, I raise up to You family and friends and those in my heart and on my mind this morning. I ask You to be with them and to meet them where they are and make Your goodness and hope known to them in real and specific ways each of them can recognize and even embrace.

Remind each of us today that our hope is about You; it is steeped in You and in Your promises. We wait on You and that act is the basis of true hope. Like love, hope in You is more than what the world describes and it is based on what You are able to do and not on our actions or abilities. We can hope in You because we have a record of who You are and all You've done and we also have Your promises of what still is to come in and through You. May that hope carry me through today and help me to love You and others with all my heart, mind, soul, and strength.

In Jesus' name I pray, Amen.

~ Day 11 ~

GOD, YOU CHOSE ME

Thank You good and gracious God, for choosing me. What a gift indeed it is to know You and to be known by You! That You know my heart and my thoughts and my concerns instills in me both confidence and joy. That You invite me to share all of these things with You, the Creator of the Universe, is indeed amazing. You provide me the opportunity and even encourage me to dump all my cares and concerns on You. You promise me peace and I am grateful for that. Even so, I am struggling to find the peace You offer in exchange for my worries and anxieties. Help me, God, to overcome my unbelief because right now it is large and looming and overwhelming me.

Even so, I know You are in control. Everything I have is Yours. Forgive me, God, for not being the good steward I am intended and supposed to be. I know You forgive me and I believe You can help me do better. Help me, please, I pray. Lord, help me overcome my unbelief.

God, I don't know how to budget our money. I don't know what to do right now. I feel paralyzed and unable to plan or even think about things like car repairs or meal plans or bills we need to pay or myriad other cares and concerns. My brain is buzzing and my emotions feel raw, as if the tears I so often try to ignore or squelch are finally going to pour down my cheeks. God, help me overcome my unbelief.

Lord, I cannot find or form the words I need to pray. I cannot express my heart or my concerns but I can feel them in my body. Help me, God, to overcome my unbelief and to trust You with all the things happening right now. Help me, help me, help me overcome my unbelief.

I know You are faithful. I know Your promises are true. I know You are the same yesterday, today, and tomorrow. I know nothing can separate me from Your love. I know You care deeply for me. I know You hear my heart and my prayers. I know you chose me.

God, You chose me. You have a plan for me and my family and each of our lives. Help me to hear from Your Holy Spirit and to trust You with today. Remind me that You will provide me with what I need for today. Help me, God, to overcome my unbelief.

I ask all these things in Jesus' name, Amen.

~ Day 12 ~

HELP ME GLORIFY YOU

Oh good and gracious God, Creator of heaven and earth, thank You for the gift of this new day and for my opportunity to come here into Your presence and seek You, to cast my cares on You, to ask You for help and wisdom and guidance. You are a God who cares deeply and intimately for Your children, including me. I know You see me. I know You know my heart. I know Your ways are not my ways and I know Your thoughts are not my thoughts.

Still, I struggle to cast my cares on You. I struggle to see anything except the things I cannot change or control right now. God, I am tightly wound and emotionally stretched and really not sure what to do. I cannot seem to focus on You rather than the storm of my circumstances right now. I want to get out of the boat, Lord. I want to walk upon the water. I want to trust You and yet my faith is shaky and too easily shaken to the point where I sink. Like Peter, I cannot keep my eyes on You. Help me, God. I feel desperate, so desperate, to fix things I cannot fix.

I hate how weak I feel and am. I hate this place of being stuck and unable to fix things on my own. Please, God, help me. Help me glorify You in my life, in my choices, in my words, in my relationships, in my prayers, in my faith. Help me overcome my unbelief. Help me trust You deeply and to know You are at work in these circumstances.

Right now, God, I want to lift up those in my heart and on my mind, friends and family who need to hear from You today and who need to feel Your hands on their shoulders and Your presence in their hearts and to sense Your presence with them in all their moments and their circumstances. God, I lift up to You (insert the names for whom you wish to pray). God, this list could go on and on and I am grateful because You know each and every one of these people and You know what they need even before they do. God, pour out Your grace and mercy and peace over each of these people and their families. Give them ears to hear from You and eyes to see You at work in and around their lives, and bend their hearts toward You. Be their strength in their weakness and be their wisdom for decisions and provide them room to pause before responding to others. Provide them room for rest and renewal. Thank You, God, for what You are going to do for each of these folks today.

In Jesus' name I pray, Amen.

~ Day 13 ~

GRATEFUL & AMAZED

Oh Lord my God, King of the Universe, I hope and pray that I will always be both grateful and amazed at the things You do and the ways You show up in my life. Lord God, You are indeed an awesome God who is Holy and righteous and just, and yet You stoop low to be a part of our lives here in this broken and messy world. You sent Your Son, Jesus Christ, into this world as a helpless, humble baby; He gave up His throne and His glory to come into this world and reveal You and Your character to us, to walk among us, and to remove the barriers that kept us apart from You. And You are still doing those things today—making a way before us and providing us glimpses of Your glory and Yourself, at work here in our lives, in my life.

God, I am indeed grateful and amazed as I watch the way You are working in our circumstances to provide us with the things we need and to create ways to help us address the things we need to address. Thank You for helping us stay focused on You and what You are able to do, which truly is far greater than we can ask or imagine.

Lord, thank You for Your faithfulness. Thank You for Your nearness. Thank You for Your promises.

This morning as I sit in Your presence I ask You to help me know You more and more. Grant me understanding and an ability to see you, really and truly see You — Your character and Your righteousness and Your love.

I also pray that those in my heart and mind and life will witness and experience these things as well. I pray You will draw them near to You and pour out Your love, Your hope, Your grace, and Your mercy over them. Touch their hearts and their lives with Your presence, revealing Yourself in the ways they can see and acknowledge and understand. Make a way for them to see You at work in their circumstances today, God.

Lord, this morning I pray for the list of people in my daily prayers (name those for whom you would like to pray), asking You to be with each and every one of them and making a way for each of them through the day today.

I thank You for all You are already doing and I continue to seek Your hand in each of their lives, continuing to provide Your goodness and mercy and grace and wisdom in all each of us does today. Thank You, God, that You are good.

I pray all these things in Jesus' name, Amen.

~ Day 14 ~

SPIRIT OF LOVE

Good and gracious God, good morning and thank You for waking me up this morning and for the gift of this day set before me. I am focusing on Your words in 2 Timothy 1:7 that tell me You have not given me a spirit of fear but a spirit of power, love, and sound judgment. Thank You for these words and for their Truth that I can rely on as I move through the day today. Help me to see this Truth at work in me today and at work in the day and in my interactions with others.

More than anything I want to see the spirit of love at work in my life today. I want to override my natural inclinations of anxiety and worry and instead embrace the power, love, and sound judgment You have placed within me. I confess, Lord, I do not focus on this much at all. I am too preoccupied with the things I want to accomplish and who I want to be in the sight of others.

I admit this is not a healthy way to live my life, and I pray Your Spirit will help to unravel that need from my tight grip. I know You have something better for me and I do acknowledge that in these prayers. But in my daily living and activities, I am still prone to proving myself worthy or successful or something else I cannot even put words to. Help me, God, truly to see myself through Your eyes and from Your eternal perspective. Help me to see eternity and to understand how to focus on the things above and the things of eternal value.

I have thoughts and ideas swirling through and around my mind; help me to take them captive today for Christ. Help me to create plans that include and involve You and Your eternal perspective and perfect plan. Help me to hear and to recognize Your Spirit as He moves in my life and whispers Truth to me and nudges me in the direction of the right paths for Your name's sake. I am unsettled about things I believe I need to address; remind me today You are in control.

It's not that I don't think goals are helpful, but I do believe sometimes they tend to draw my attention from You as I work in my own strength and according to my own plans and ideas to complete goals I have not formed in partnership with You. I am still running down the path, God, calling back to You to bless my efforts rather than walking with You or, even more, following You. Help me today to walk more intentionally with You and to seek the things above. Help me today to respond to Your Spirit. I love You, Lord. Thank you for who You are and what You are doing in my life.

In Jesus' name I pray, Amen.

~ Day 15 ~

THE DAY YOU MADE

Oh good and gracious God, You are the King of the Universe and the Lord of all Creation, and I am grateful to You for waking me up this morning and inviting me into Your presence to sit with You and to receive from You the blessings of love and grace and wisdom You so generously pour into me. Thank You, Father, for the opportunity and the privilege to know You and to be known by You. As I sit here, I breathe deeply Your peace and Your comfort. I rest in You and confess You as my refuge and my strength. You see me and You know the challenges before me and You are generous in equipping me for what I need to do, and You also remind me I do not face anything on my own, but that You go before me and with me and You make a way for me in this, the day You have made.

God, please be with me deep in my soul and spirit and speak to me about next steps for my family and for me. Provide me wisdom and a sense of clarity for possibilities ahead for us, wherever that leads. I turn to You and seek You. I request wisdom and understanding in the midst of difficult or overwhelming circumstances and I trust You to answer me because I know You care deeply about us and for us. I trust Your plans and Your Will more than my own and I ask You to speak, Lord, for Your servant is listening. Help make space for me to listen and to hear from You today, God. Remind me to pause and to seek you throughout the day.

This morning I also raise up to You those in my heart and those on my mind. I pray You will meet each person where they are and meet their needs, providing those things You know they need for today. May Your still, small voice be the one they hear and heed today. I pray this for (insert the names for whom you wish to pray). I am grateful because You know the names and the needs of all those in my heart and on my mind. Meet them where they are and walk through their day with them today, Lord, the day You have made. I thank You, God, for who You are and all that You are going to do today in my life and the lives of each of those for whom I pray.

I ask all these things in Jesus' name, Amen.

~ Day 16 ~

MY GOOD & YOUR GLORY

Good morning, good and gracious and loving God. What a joy and blessing it is to meet You here this morning. How I look forward to this time in Your presence because, when I am here in the morning stillness, with the day dawning outside my window, I am quickly reminded of who You are. Your creativity is on display all around me and the works of Your hand testify to Your goodness and Your lovingkindness and they strike wonder and awe in my heart. As I read Your Word this morning, I am grateful for the reminder that You are never far from me and Your Holy Spirit is indeed my comforter and my guide. Again, I am deeply grateful for this because I have known what it is like to wander lost and alone in the darkness of circumstances or fear. I am grateful and relieved that I do not have to move through this world or my day and its challenges alone. Rather You go out before me to make a way for me and You go with me to strengthen me and encourage me. I know I will face nothing today for which You cannot equip me to face alongside You.

Thank You, God, for not leaving me alone.

Thank You for Your promises that prove true every day.

Thank You for Your steadfastness and deep care for me.

Thank You for working everything, every circumstance, including every trial, for my good and Your glory. And today, God, I invite You to reveal to me where You are at work in me and in my life. Use Your Holy Spirit's dwelling within me to refine me and guide me into the good things, like my response to adversity and the way I speak to those in my life. Help me through Your Holy Spirit to more fully reflect You—Your grace and Your mercy, Your love and Your glory—to my family, to my friends, and to all those with whom I interact today, because I confess, God, too often lately, when I have forgone this time with You, I have been more ornery, more afraid, and more likely to give in to my selfishness and my anger and my fear.

Thank You for showing me a better way, God, in the life and ministry of Jesus. Thank You for providing me a better way in Christ. Please forgive me when I want to nurse my anger or hold tightly to a grudge. Today, I invite You to work all the things in my circumstances, including whatever insults or hurts or judgments from others, work them all together for my good and Your glory. Help me today to trust You even more than yesterday.

God, I also invite You to reveal to me where I need to change and to help me release the things I need to let go of in order to better serve You and to become more like You.

Thank You, Heavenly Father, for the grace and mercy You pour over me. Thank You for the forgiveness of my sins, for my shortcomings, and for all the ways I have missed the mark set before me—missed good works or missed tasks not completed or missed opportunities to extend grace to others. Help me today to do better and to be better.

God, I lift up to You friends and family and all those in my heart and in my mind, including all those I name regularly (name all those for whom you want to pray today). Be with them and meet them where they are today. Lead them and guide them and provide for them the things they need. Even more, reveal Yourself to each of them in the ways they will see and understand and receive. Soften their hearts, Lord, bending them more and more toward You.

I pray all these things in Jesus' name, Amen.

~ Day 17 ~

TRUE FAITH & GRATITUDE

Good and gracious and mighty God, You are the Creator, King of the Universe. Through You all things were made and by Your mighty right hand, all things are upheld and maintained. In fact, it is in You, oh Lord, that I live and move and have my being. Reveal to me today, Lord, what these words truly mean — show me how it is in You that I have these things. Grant me a deeper and truer understanding of this Truth and help me to apply it to my life today according to Your will and Your ways and not mine.

Lord God, grant me today a deep and authentic faith and gratitude; let them be a deeper faith and a gratitude that transcends my circumstances and my weak and human ways and thoughts. Thank You, God, that Your ways are not my ways and Your thoughts are not my thoughts; let today be a day wherein I witness You and Your goodness in obvious ways. Reveal Yourself to me and provide me a true faith, not a cursory or surface faith that I then present or project to the world and that is more show than substance.

Today, Lord, I invite You to refine my thoughts and my perspective and to shape my ways so they resemble more of You and who You are. I want to exude and reflect true faith and gratitude. I confess, God, sometimes I fight hard to be grateful. I fight my natural inclination to complain or to wallow. I fight my natural human desire to submit to and embrace my anger or sense of what is fair. Today, God, let Your Holy Spirit refine and reform me like clay in Your Potter's hands.

This morning I also pray for all those in my heart and on my mind, asking You to walk closely with each of them and whispering Your truth and Your hope to them in every moment and circumstance. I pray for those who are struggling today, that they will sense You with them and You will indeed be their refuge and their strength. I pray this especially for (insert the names for whom you wish to pray). Be their strength and their stronghold today.

God, I thank You for who You are and all the things You are going to do today in the lives of each of these folks and in mine. I ask You for health and healing and wholeness. I ask You to help me trust You no matter what and I commit my ideas, my projects, and my whole day to You. I commit my gifts and abilities to You, giving back to You the gifts You entrusted to me to use for Your glory. Help me to be bold and courageous and to work at my tasks with a sense of joy and purpose always.

I pray all these things in Jesus' name, Amen.

~ Day 18 ~

GOOD AND GRACIOUS

Good morning my good and gracious Lord and Savior. How I love those two words and even more how I love to speak them each morning when I say good morning to You, good and gracious God. For You are the King of the Universe and the One True God, and like C.S. Lewis wrote about Aslan, "of course he isn't safe, but he's good." You are Holy and mighty and no one can see Your face and live, and yet You invite us into Your presence again and again. You work all things out for our good because You are good. You indeed are good and gracious, pouring out Your grace in great abundance again and again when we fall short of Your commands.

Lord, help me today to be good and gracious. To be loving and kind. To be a truer reflection of You than of myself. Help me, God, to embody who You are and who You are calling me to be today. Let my words and my ways today look more like You than me. Let me be a light of hope and of no-matter-what love in the world today.

Thank You, Lord, for the gift of today and for the rest You provided me. Thank You for hearing my prayer and responding with an abundance of goodness.

This morning I lift up to You friends and family and others who are in my heart and on my mind (name those for whom you want to pray). Thank You for who You are and what You are going to do in the lives of each of these people because You know what they need and You promise to provide each of us what we need each day. Be with those who are hurting and grieving, comfort the broken-hearted and bring healing to those who are sick. You are the One who can cure even the seemingly impossible-to-cure diseases and illnesses and bring strength to the weary. May You do that and more today for each of these I lift up to You (name those for whom you wish to pray). And for all those who are in my sphere and who need to see glimpses of You at work in their lives and in the world today, reveal Yourself to them in the ways they can understand and experience in real ways. Let me, too, be a vessel through which You reach Your people today.

Thank You, good and gracious God for who You are and all You are going to do today in my life and the lives of all these named and unnamed here. And help me to follow Your Word and to live it out in powerful ways today.

In Jesus' name I pray these things, Amen.

~ Day 19 ~

LOVING OTHERS AS YOU DO

Good and gracious God, as I come into Your presence this morning, I am angry and overwhelmed by life and the circumstances where we are. I want to shake my fist and stomp my feet and yell at the heavens about the unfairness I feel is at work in my life. But I also confess that I experience nothing less than what Jesus experienced in the world; I acknowledge that there is nothing I go through that Jesus doesn't understand and that He Himself didn't experience or endure. With this in mind, I ask You to help me, Lord, to help me see things in my life through Your eyes and Your eternal perspective because I confess that is difficult for me right now. I want life to be easier. I want circumstances to be less stressful or anxiety-invoking. I want to have days that feel easier.

But I also know that what I truly want and need is You.

I want and need a deeper and stronger faith. I want and need an out-of-the-boat, walk-on-the-waves faith. The kind of faith that requires me to keep my eyes on You and not on the stormy gales of my circumstances that sometimes feels like the lack of support I think I need and then seek from others, from the world, and not from You.

God, I don't get how life works sometimes. Truly, I don't. I try to cast a net far and deep when You tell me to do so. And I try to step out in faith upon the waves of the storm, trusting You to make big things happen. And when those big things don't happen, I lose my trust and I take my eyes off You and within moments I falter and sink, losing confidence in my ideas and plans I felt assured I had worked out with You.

Help me, God, to see my life through fresh eyes. Help me to pause and to breathe and to trust You. Shore me up in my faith today, God, by Your Holy Spirit. Help me to lean on You and not on my own understanding, my faulty and weak understanding. Today, at some point, I am going to do the big things and use the gifts You have given me because I do believe I have gifts and talents You provided me and I want to use them to glorify You. Lord, help me to find the place for my talent by making the way. Your will be done, not mine.

And God, I hear today's verse about living and praying for those who hurt and mistreat you, and I humbly ask You to soften my heart toward those who have disappointed or hurt me. I want to embody the posture of Christ despite how hard that is for my finite human mind to do so. Help me to pray for and to love them in Your no-matter-what kind of loving approach because You know and can see how much I don't want to and how much I want to hold on to my perceived righteousness and human response of stoicism and stubbornness.

Forgive me, God, for this response and help me to overcome my instinctive ways of being.

Lord, there are also circumstances that are hard right now (name your specific concerns and lay them in God's capable hands). I am casting all these concerns on You and asking for You to strengthen me and to help me not to worry and fret as I am wont to do. Help me to embrace Your ways, the ways described and prescribed in Your word.

I pray all these things in Jesus' name, Amen.

~ Day 20 ~

THE GOD WHO SEES ME

Oh good and gracious God, Lord of lords and King of kings, thank You for the gift of this beautiful brand new day. Thank You for calling me forth from my sleep and for providing me with the opportunity to come and sit with You. Thank You for being the God who sees me and the God who hears me, and the God who loves me no matter what. Help me today to focus on You and wanting to please You rather than wanting to be lauded by my fellow human beings in this world. Help me remember, Father, that my life in You is the true treasure of this life, not the approval of man or Facebook or social media or friends or family. I acknowledge that too often I am focused on what I can write or post or create in order to gain some kind of traction on a social media platform to impress others. Remind me and help me today to live my life for You. This is something that truly matters to me but I realize my actions too often do not reflect my desire to live for and to please You.

By Your Holy Spirit today, keep my feet on the path You have set before me and my eyes focused on the good works You have designed specifically for me and given me to complete. Provide me a deep and true understanding of what that means so that these are not merely words I pray, but are matters that shift my heart, softening it and bending it more and more towards You as the One who loves me no matter what, the One who sees me, and the One who hears me.

Lord, this morning I raise up to You those who are hurting and those who are sick and in need of Your healing touch to restore them to wholeness. Be with all those who are unwell or sick in various ways today, whether with a virus or with more serious and chronic illness and pain. Relieve them from their pain and sickness and help each of them hold fast to You today.

I also raise up to You those who are grieving or suffering in the face of loss or hurt, whether physical, emotional, or mental. Be with those who have lost loved ones or friends or even trusted and loved family pets. Be with those who have lost their homes and everything they once had and treasured because of storms or fires or from accidents. Comfort those whose burdens are crushing and too much for them to bear. Help them to see You with them in the darkness of loss and grief.

I also raise up to You those who are facing challenges and difficulties in relationships or in work or school or in life overall. You are a God of comfort and compassion and a God who sees and cares for each of us on a deeply personal level. You care about even the smallest details of our lives, and I pray You will be with each of those who are wrestling with uncertainty or hurt and guide them closer to You where they can know Your no-matter-what kind of love today and take comfort in Your arms and Your hope and strength.

God, please hear my prayer for all those in need of You today and place Your hand upon them in mighty ways, drawing them closer to You and revealing Yourself to them in real and powerful ways they can see and understand and recognize as You.

I pray all these things for my friends and family today in Jesus' name, Amen.

~ Day 21 ~

EVEN NOW

Good morning, good and gracious and holy God, King of the Universe. As I raise my eyes to the heavens, even now I am awed by the fact that You are here and I am awed by the nearness of You and the presence of You here with me. Even now, I marvel at the works of Your hands and am stirred to worship You as I consider that You placed the stars into the sky and spoke the Universe into existence. Even now, I am comforted by the knowledge that You hold everything together and that my life truly matters to You and all of its details are in Your hands. Even now, as I observe the early morning sky shift from hues of orange and pink into the full light of day, I am reminded of

Your perfect timing and the incredible creativity with which You have breathed life into this world and drawn each of us flawed and imperfect human beings in Your perfect and holy image, redeeming us by Christ's perfect sacrifice. Even now, I rejoice in knowing You, giving You thanks and joining with the songs of the birds and all creation to praise You and acknowledge You as the God of my moments.

Thank You, Lord, for who You are and for who I am in and with and through You. Thank You for a new day and Your presence with me even now as things get underway. Thank You for calling me forth into today and for all You are going to do for me and through me today. Even now as I sit in Your presence I present myself as a living sacrifice as Paul wrote in his letter to the Romans:

"Therefore, brothers and sisters, in view of the mercies of God, I urge you to present your bodies as a living sacrifice, holy and pleasing to God; this is your true worship." God, help me to live this out in my life today. Help me to live as one consecrated and set apart for

You because that is what is deeply true. You have called me and consecrated me and set me apart for Yourself and I want to reflect that in my thoughts, words, and actions. I know Your words are true, and, even now, I have before me opportunities and possibilities created by You just for me because in You I live and move and have my being. My every breath comes from You. Let my life honor and glorify You today. Let the work of my hands and words of my mouth reflect Your grace, Your no-matter-what love, and Your deep care for the people in Your world.

Even now, God, I thank You for all You are going to do today, and I pray all these things in Jesus' name, Amen.

~ Day 22 ~

EVERY GOOD & PERFECT GIFT

Good morning, good and gracious and loving God. How great it is to come into Your presence and how awesome You are to behold at work in the world and in my life each day. Help me today, God, to fix my eyes and my thoughts on You. Help me to keep my mind's focus on who You are and the attributes that make You the good and gracious and holy God You are. Thank You today for the reminder in Your Word that no matter the state of the world or the circumstances of my life, You have created and placed good things in the world for me to see and to be encouraged and inspired by—whether in nature, like the songs of the birds or the changing color of the leaves, or in people I encounter or already know, like in church listening to a sermon from our pastor or in a phone conversation with a trusted friend. Thank You also for the reminder that every good and perfect gift is from You. Open my eyes to those good and perfect gifts and to Your presence with me in each moment and task set before me today.

God, you are merciful and kind and worthy to be praised. Let my life be lived in praise of You. Let my mind focus upon and stay steadfast in the pursuit of You and Your goodness because I confess that too often I am easily distracted by the noise of the world, and today I want my life to be in Your hands from now until I lay my head down upon the pillow.

Oh Lord, lead me and guide me in the ways I can support those I love and care for. Show me ways to encourage them and help me to help them uncover their gifts and talents and abilities and to put those to use to make a way in this world for themselves and others and also to honor You, the Giver of those good and perfect gifts.

I confess, God, that the days often feel too short and too busy to do anything real or anything of consequence. But I know and acknowledge before You right now that thoughts like that are lies from the enemy, who seeks to keep me stuck and mired in unbelief and distract me from Your goodness and Your mercy and Your generous provision for me. I lose sight of You and Your promises when the enemy's lies overtake my thoughts and that is why I seek You right now, Father, because I want You to be my specific focus today. I want to surrender my life to You as a living sacrifice who is given the opportunity to choose for myself what I will do with my will and my thoughts and my day, and I choose in this quiet and still moment to follow You wherever You lead me today.

I have some things I'd like to work on today and I raise those up to You right now and ask You to guide me in my efforts in each of those projects, in the creating of creative and sacred spaces here in my home and in considering the ways You provide what we need each day. God, I know You are faithful in all You do and You will bring to completion the work You begin in us—You equip and empower and You pour out wisdom generously when we ask, and so I am asking for Your wisdom and Your provision.

Open my eyes today to the work You are doing in me and through me and give me ears to hear and a mind to understand what You have for me to do today. And when I lose my way as I am prone and likely to do in the midst of the day's noise and busyness and distractions, bring me back to this place in heart and mind by the power and wisdom and guidance of Your Holy Spirit so that I do not lose sight or focus on You today. Remind me to pause; and equip and empower me to bring You honor and glory in my thoughts, words, and actions today.

In Jesus' name I pray these things, Amen.

~ Day 23 ~

LISTEN TO MY PRAYER

Oh good and gracious God, I come before You this morning with my heart somewhat heavy and my mind full of questions and concerns and my heart desiring You and that Your will be done in all things today. With that in mind, I include the words of David as part of my prayers this morning:

"God, listen to my prayer and do not hide from my plea for help" (Psalm 55:1 CSB).

Lord God, I lay before You our finances and our need to be better stewards and also to find ways to increase our income and to cover our bills each month. God, listen to my prayer and do not hide from my plea for help.

Lord God, I seek Your input and guidance when it comes to the tasks and work set before me today. Help me to know what it is You would have me do today. God, listen to my prayer and do not hide from my plea for help.

Lord God, go out before me and my family and friends and make the way You want us to travel. Provide each of us with open minds and open hearts to do the work necessary to move us forward to become the people You created and designed us to be. Bring out our gifts and talents and abilities and help us discover our path in the world as designed by You. God, listen to my prayer and do not hide from my plea for help.

Lord God, be a part of all the moments of my day and especially of the work You place in my hands and the good works You created for me to do so long ago. Help make me successful and create opportunities for me to reflect You and bring Your Kingdom according to Your plan. God, listen to my prayer and do not hide from my plea for help.

Lord God, make a way for me and help clarify my vision and the details of the work of my hands. Relieve me of any anxiety or critical perspective of my efforts and to embrace the process of exploration and curiosity that will help bring my story to life in Your hands. God, listen to my prayer and do not hide from my plea for help.

Lord God, help me when I am frozen or stuck and uncertain about what to do with things in our home or my life as I work to declutter and organize my life as a creative space where You can work in me and in those I love. God, listen to my prayer and do not hide from my plea for help.

And finally, Lord God, reveal to me how I can be an instrument of change for You in Your world, this world that You created and spoke into existence with love and with exquisite creativity. Use me to glorify You, to honor You, to reveal and reflect You to those around me. The world so often feels dark and divided, but Jesus overcame the darkness and even death in His sacrificial life and death and resurrection. Help me to be a light in whatever ways You need me to do so today. God, listen to my prayer and do not hide from my plea for help.

I pray all these things in Jesus' name, Amen.

~ Day 24 ~

SPEAK AND I WILL LISTEN

Oh good and gracious God, how grateful I am to come into Your presence this morning. Thank You for this opportunity to begin again and to shed the weight of my thoughts and my concerns here in Your presence. I come seeking and hoping and desperately wanting to hear from You, inviting You to speak into my life and into my selfishness in order to provide me the strength and ability with which to shift my selfish, self-centered perspective to a more selfless and surrendered one. I confess to You, Lord, that I am too easily influenced toward indulgence and selfishness and I ask You to forgive me for that and also to move me from that place.

Lord, I invite You to speak into my life and into my heart. I invite You to speak and also ask You to provide me with the ability to hear You and to follow You. I am deeply grateful to You for the words in Colossians 2:9 this morning—"For the entire fullness of God's nature dwells bodily in Christ"—because I know that as I read the New Testament I am receiving glimpses of You in Jesus and through his actions and interactions with those with whom He crossed paths as well as those with whom He shared His days and His life and His meals. God, how I want to be like one of His apostles, learning from Him and growing in understanding and abounding in grace and love. I know they got it wrong sometimes, too, but I want to be better than I am right now, God. I want to be a better version of myself according to Your will and Your plans.

And so I invite You to speak into my life today. I invite You to go before me and with me and I give You permission to overhaul my ways in favor of Yours. I give You a blank check of faith to do in my life what You know to be the things I need and that will benefit me the greatest. Speak, and I will listen, Lord, because I want my life to be a reflection of who You are in all Your goodness and grace and mercy and love. I want to embody hope. And I want to be like the 11 faithful apostles who gave up everything and followed Jesus and even still sometimes got it wrong or didn't understand but who were committed to Christ.

Let that be my legacy for this day, Lord.

I pray this in Jesus' name, Amen.

~ Day 25 ~

BE THOU MY VISION

Good and gracious God, I am grateful to be in Your presence this morning because for reasons unknown to me I woke up in worry and uncertainty and feeling out of sorts before my eyes were even all the way open. For unknown reasons my mind raced to anxieties and concerns and a feeling of having already been defeated this morning and so I sought You in those first moments and I seek You now. I seek to know You and Your presence in this very moment and I seek to pour out my cares and exchange them for Your perfect peace.

Psalm 34:19 says even one who is righteous will have many adversities, but You, oh God, will rescue him from every one. And so, dear

Father, I look to You, not as one who is righteous by my efforts or on my own, but as one who has been made righteous and is continually made righteous each moment by Your Son and my Savior Jesus Christ. I look to You in this moment to rescue me from my thinking and my overwhelm; from my thinking that things are already askew and out of control. I acknowledge that so many things truly are out of my control but my thoughts and my desires are not. I can take each of them captive to Christ and that is what I do right now.

Right now I lean into You and I lift my eyes to the heavens, and, as I do, I ask You to be thou my vision—be the focus of my eyes and my mind and my heart. Be the focus of my thoughts and provide me the vision for my day and for my remaining days as well. I acknowledge You are in control and nothing surprises You. Therefore, I know I am in good Hands and You will keep me in perfect peace no matter my circumstances as long as I keep my eyes and my mind on You.

Lord, thank You for today. Thank You for Your new mercies and Your ever-present presence and for Your no-matter-what love that pours over me and fills me to overflowing. I can do all things through You who provides me strength and vision.

Lord, open my eyes to the opportunities and possibilities You are setting before me today, and use Your Holy Spirit to spur me onward in the direction of the vision You provide me this morning. Help me to cleave to You whatever happens today.

And this morning, I also lift up to You those in my heart and on my mind and ask You to be with each person and reveal Yourself to them in specific ways that they will realize and understand and that they will draw nearer to You as a result (insert the names of those for whom you wish to pray today). Thank You, God, for all that You are going to do today in their lives as well as in mine.

I pray all these things in Jesus' name, Amen.

~ Day 26 ~

ANOINTING AND MEALS BY YOU

Good morning, good and gracious God. I am here in Your presence this morning filled with worries and concerns but wanting to release those and cast them on You. But we both know how challenging a task that is for me and what broken soundtracks I have created for myself in wanting to control aspects of my life that in reality are not mine to control. Lord, I am constantly anxious despite my wanting to trust You. And so I pray this morning and ask You to help me.

I ask You to remind me there is nowhere I will go today, nowhere You are not with me. You know what this day holds and You know what is coming up for me not only today but in the days and weeks ahead. Lord, I need to trust You, but I also believe I am meant to participate *with* You. Reveal to me what that looks like. Show me the path as we walk through the day together.

Your Word from David tells me about You preparing him a meal and anointing his head with oil, and, Lord, that is what I crave. I want Your anointing and I want the meals You promise to prepare in the presence of my enemies, even and especially when that enemy is my fear and my doubt, whispered by the father of lies.

Help me today to trust You more. Help me to listen for Your whispers of truth and direction and to respond to them in true and authentic faith.

Help me to come to the table You have prepared and to recline at that table with You, as the disciples did when they shared meals with Jesus, even on the night of His death. Grant me a vision of Your hand at work in my life. God, it is so incredibly difficult for me not to obsess over my worries. Even so, I want to trust You. I want to put my faith in You and Your promises because I know You indeed care for me and are interested in even the smallest of details in my life.

God, guide me today I pray, in Jesus' name, Amen.

~ Day 27 ~

YOU ENCOURAGE ME

Good and gracious God, King of the Universe, thank You for the gift of this wonderful new day. Thank You for choosing me and for loving me and for inviting me into Your presence to talk to you, to lay my burdens down at Your feet and to experience Your perfect peace in their place. You encourage me each day, God, to walk with You and to follow where You lead and once again this morning I am eager to do so. I am eager to hear from You and to receive Your wisdom and know Your guiding along the right paths for Your Name's sake.

You are generous and You are loving. You are intimately interested in my life and You let me know that every day when I enter Your presence with my requests. Lord, thank You for the opportunity to sit here with You. Thank You for Your love and Your faithfulness and for Your promises to never leave me nor forsake me. I am deeply grateful to You because I never walk alone. You are in the midst of all my circumstances and You are at work in me, refining me and reshaping me like clay in Your Potter's hands.

Be with me today, Lord, and guide me. Guide my steps along the path upon which You are leading me and help me to follow You. By Your Spirit, remind me to pause today to check in with You, to hear from You, and to know what You want me to do. Help me to love You and love others as Jesus instructed us to do. Help me to see the tasks set before me as a way to honor You because, when I serve others, I know I am serving You.

God, this morning I also want to take a moment to lift up to You those in my life and in my heart and on my mind. I ask You to be with each of them and to reveal Yourself to them.

Help them to see You and to recognize You in their lives as You draw them nearer and nearer to You. Be their healer where they need one. Be their wisdom-giver. Be their strength and refuge when they need it. Be their grace and their mercy and pour out Your provision according to Your perfect timing, perfect will, and perfect plan.

God, I pray all these things in Jesus' name, Amen.

~ Day 28 ~

LOOKED AFTER AND CROWNED WITH GLORY

Good morning, good and gracious God. Thank You for waking me up this morning and for providing me this gift of another day with its opportunities and possibilities. Thank You for the truth that You do not change and You are the same yesterday, today, and forever and I can know You through Your Word. Thank You for making the way through Jesus Christ, Your Son and my Savior, to be reconciled to You, reconciled and redeemed.

"What is a human being that You remember him, a son of man that You look after him? You made him little less than God and crowned him with glory and honor" (Psalm 8:4-5 CSB).

Thank You, God, for these words, for the reminder that I am not only looked after but also crowned with glory and with honor. As I reflect on these words, I am overwhelmed by their meaning and by the deep love and care they portray for me. Not only am I never alone, but I am looked after and crowned with glory. How can I view myself as anything less than when I contemplate the Truth in Your Word each morning? Your love overwhelms me and Your care for even the smallest details of my life inspires me to come into Your presence again and again to worship You and shower You with my praise and my gratitude.

Today, Lord, I come before Your throne of grace and lay down my agenda and my expectations. I surrender all of me to all of You because I want Your absolute best for me, Your abundant life and Your joy and Your strength and Your mercy and Your grace. I want to bask in Your loving presence and I want You to align my heart with Yours so Your desires are my desires; only then will I ask You to give me my heart's desires, only when they are Yours poured into me.

Let my mind be Yours. Let my heart be Yours. Let my desires be Yours. Today, Lord, let me be obedient to You and to trust You to do what You say You will do for me. Thank You for what You are going to do today in my life as You continue to refine me and mold me more and more into Your image.

I pray these things in Jesus' name, Amen.

~ Day 29 ~

PEACE IN ALL THINGS

Oh good and gracious and perfect God, You are the one who calms the storms that churn the seas and that churn in me. You spoke and the wind abated and the waves calmed and the disciples marveled. You are that same God still today and we call on Your name to calm the storms that bear down on us today, whether actual storms or emotional, chaotic ones, stirred within us and our lives. Provide Your hand of protection and pour out Your peace over each of those who face uncertainty or fear or any storms in this life. We know nothing is impossible for You and so we ask You to turn back the storms of our lives like Jesus did on the sea with His disciples; weaken the ferocity and lessen any damage in the storm's path.

Lord God, I also seek You this morning to work in my life and in my day here with my family and those I love. Be with us as we work to serve You by serving others in big and small ways. Provide us perspective and gratitude today and the ability to acknowledge our many blessings. Help us, God, to support our community, our state, our nation through prayers and acts of kindness and service. Help us discover balance in overwhelming circumstances and to then provide support to others because we have walked a similar path and are able to pour compassion and strength into the journeys of those in our community.

God, You are good and You are Holy and You made a way for us to know You and be in a relationship with You. Today I want to honor You in my thoughts, my words, and my actions. Today, I invite You to work in me and refine me, and to align my heart with Yours so that the desires of my heart are Your desires. And I invite You to use me to be a light of hope in a world desperate to know You and Your love.

God, I pray these things in Jesus' name, Amen.

~ Day 30 ~

GREEN PASTURES & QUIET WATERS

Day after day, good and gracious God, You bear my burdens and You are my salvation. How can my heart and mind not praise You? How can I not lift Your name and bless You? How great thou art and how mighty a God You are who watches over us and wants to know us through a daily relationship. Nothing is too difficult for You and nothing surprises You either. You see into my life and nothing scares You off or leads You to leave me—talk about amazing grace indeed!

Oh good and gracious God, how grateful I am this morning to meet with You and to share this time together. You are generous and loving and I am in need of Your renewal and grace this morning as I look ahead at the day. I feel a bit more tired than I would like this morning, but I know and trust You as the source of my strength and my provision today. You invite me into green pastures and beside quiet waters and You promise to restore my soul and renew my mind and to anoint my head with oil, a sign of Your deep and real acceptance of me. Thank You, God, for meeting me here this morning and for being a God of goodness and love and justice. Thank You for making me whole and holy. Thank You for loving me.

This morning I raise up to You friends and family and others who are in my heart and on my mind. I ask You to meet them where they are this morning and to make Yourself real and known to them, to provide them glimpses of You and the work You are doing in them and their lives and through them in their parts of the world. Bring comfort and strength to those who are struggling or doubting today (insert the names of those for whom you are praying).

God, meet each person for whom I pray where they are and guide them into the good works You designed specifically for them. Help them to see You in the world and at work around them.

May there be comfort and healing and strength and wholeness and a sense of You for each of them. May we each strive to love You and serve You today. May we also strive to love and serve our neighbors as well as strangers who cross our paths.

You are a God of unity and goodness and not a God of chaos or division. I pray for those newly elected and ask You to be the wisdom and goodness and unifying presence we need in order to create healing and peace among us. Give them the strength they need and the desire required to do the right thing, to be true servants who work for all people, the good of all people, and for justice as You bring it to bear in this world.

God, thank You for who You are and all You are going to do in my life and in the world today. I lift up those for whom I pray daily and ask You to walk with them through whatever circumstances they face. Thank you.

I pray all these things in Jesus' name, Amen.

~ Day 31 ~

GOD'S GRACE & TRUTH

Oh good and gracious God, thank You for this morning and the time I get to spend with You. Thank You for the reminder in the early morning light that it is not only the morning or the day that is new but so are Your mercies and because of that I am invited to a clean-slate of a day. Yesterday's stumbles and shortcomings are forgiven and matter not this morning as I sit here and surrender the coming day to You. I pray right now, Lord, that Your grace and truth will pierce my heart and guide my thoughts, words, and deeds. As I move through today, open my eyes and reveal more and more to me the ways Your grace and truth have intertwined and continue to intertwine in the life of Your son and my savior, Jesus Christ. Help me to both embrace and embody this idea in my own interactions with others.

Also, God, I want You to speak Your Truth into my life and make it the central guiding principle in all I undertake today. As I move through the day ahead, I invite You to pour out Your wisdom and provide me with greater understanding of Your Truth and Your never-changing character. When I read Your Word, I ask You to pierce through the layers of wrong thoughts and pour out the burning embers of Truth and grace and mercy and understanding within me. Humble me and help me to surrender myself and my plans wholly to You.

God, when I look around the place where I am, let me see You here. Remind me through Your Creation the ways You engage with and care about this world and also about me and my life. You invite me daily to cast my cares upon You because You care for me. You are aware of even the minutest details in my life and You invite me, even command me, not to worry about anything in my life. How hard that can feel, Lord, laying my concerns at Your feet and choosing to receive Your peace in the place of my cares. But how can I serve You, how can I worship You, if I am preoccupied with myself and my concerns?

Help me today, God, to live out the words in 1 John 4:16—"And we have come to know and to believe the love that God has for us. God is love, and the one who remains in love remains in God, and God remains in him."

Help me to remain in love. Help me to trust You and to follow where You lead. Help me to reflect You and to speak to others with grace and Truth. Help me to be humble and to live surrendered in all aspects of my life today.

Lord, I love You and I invite You to refine me according to Your good purposes. I give You permission to soften the hardened edges of my thoughts and ways and I implore You to soften my heart toward You and toward others. Help me, God, to love You and to love my neighbors. Make me an instrument of Your peace and help me to take my selfish thoughts, my angry thoughts, my flawed thoughts captive to Christ today, allowing Your Holy Spirit to give me new thoughts more in line with Your truth and grace.

I pray these things in Jesus' name, Amen.

Nighttime Prayers

~ Night 1 ~

REST FOR MY SOUL

Good and gracious God, what a gift this day has been, from starting the day in Your presence this morning, to seeking Your guiding hand and wisdom over and throughout my day. Lord, right now I thank you for all this day was and for all the tasks and possibilities and opportunities You provided me. Thank You for Your care and Your wisdom, leading and guiding me in all the things You set before me today.

And now as I move into my evening, I turn to You and admit my trust in You, Lord, with me and with my rest, knowing even now You want what is best for me. As I settle into my night, I ask You to provide me glimpses of You and Your deep and intimate care for me and the many ways You were at work in my day. May I spend this time in reflection of Your love and Your hope and who You are. Be the rest for my soul and the purpose for each of my desires and dreams. Take all of me, God, hold me in Your hands, watching over me and providing me a deep and peaceful rest. Thank You for Your presence with me. I am indeed truly grateful knowing You are my refuge and You watch over me always because You never sleep.

I pray this in Jesus' name, Amen.

~ Night 2 ~

HELP ME TO CHANGE

Good and gracious God, I come to You, into Your presence tonight, because I want to talk to You before I consider sleep tonight. I want to seek Your face and Your grace and Your mercy because I need them right now, God. I need You.

I need You to help me to change—to change my ways and to change my thoughts and to change my mindset. I need more of You and less of me. I have been selfish and self-centered and I ask You to forgive me, God. I ask You to shift my heart, to soften it, to bend it toward You.

Lord, some days I cannot stand beneath the weight of the choices I make when I am overwhelmed or tired or just too filled with uncertainty or anxiety. I forget to seek You as my strength and instead rely on my own strength, which is really none at all, and I am unable to do anything that truly matters.

Lord, help me tonight to forgive myself and steep me in Your mercy and grace as I rest in You. Grant me a deep and restful sleep in Your arms. Keep me in Your protection and provide me the assurance of Your presence. Let me awaken tomorrow awash in Your love and hope, and tonight let me rest in Your perfect peace.

I pray for You to bring comfort and peace to my household as they drift into sleep. Be for all of us a calming presence, a real presence we can sense. Grant us rest in You and provide us relief from any anxiety or overwhelm or stress or uncertainties. I place each of us in Your care.

And I pray this prayer of confession and desire for change in Jesus' name, Amen.

~ Night 3 ~

RESTFUL SLEEP

Good and gracious God, I come to You tonight and thank You for the day I enjoyed today. Thank You for Your faithfulness and for Your ever-present presence with me in each and every moment of my day. As the day winds down and comes to its close, I also want to ask You for a good and deep and restful sleep for me, and for my family. Lord, it can be difficult to wrestle with anxieties or worries, and I ask You to come alongside me and be my strength and my protector in the face of my unrelenting anxieties. God, I know You are who You say You are and that Your promises are both personal and powerful and so I place my trust in You tonight as I place myself and my family in Your care. Surround us in grace and pour out Your peace over each of us tonight and give us restful sleep in Your arms.

I pray this in Jesus' name, Amen.

~ Night 4 ~

TIME TO REST

Oh Lord, my God, as I settle into my bed, I come to You and raise up my praise and thanksgiving. I also raise up to You the end of this day and thank You for all of the provision and generosity You poured over me today. I also lift up my friends and my family, asking You to watch over them and to grant them rest in You. Wash away their anxieties, cares, concerns, and fears, and in their place grant each of them Your perfect peace. Wrap all of us in the comfort of Your Holy Spirit. Release us from any intrusive thoughts or skewed perspectives and give us rest. Hold us in Your loving peace that passes all understanding as we settle down for sleep. Remove any unfounded worries and anxieties and provide instead Your hope and Your peace. Surround us with Your angel army and let Your warriors watch over us and let Your Holy Spirit surround us in His peace and presence so we may rest well tonight.

In Jesus' name I ask these things, Amen.

~ Night 5 ~

HARD DAYS & GRATITUDE

Lord God, Heavenly Father, today was a hard day and I don't feel like I have any gratitude in me and yet even as I write those words I know in the deepest part of me how much I need to praise You. What I want is to rail and rant and wallow, but what I *need* is You. What I need is to turn my eyes upon You. What I need is to thank You for who You are and for Your generosity and for Your ever-present presence with me. What I need is to admit and acknowledge and accept and embrace that even on the hard days, especially on the hard days, here You are, God with me.

And, Lord, I need that more than anything right now. Father, I need You more than anything tonight. I have struggled and I have grumbled and I have snapped and I have withdrawn. I have failed and fallen way short. And yet You are still here and You are still with me and still pouring out Your mercy and Your grace. You have not abandoned me and for that I truly am grateful. Still You love me with a deep and abiding and abundant love. Thank You.

As I seek rest and eventually sleep tonight, I thank You and I seek You. Even on my worst day, even in my worst moments, You are still God and You are still on Your throne. Still my every breath is because of You. Lord, let me rest in You tonight in Your no-matter-what love. Thank You for being with me on the hard days.

I pray this in Jesus' name, Amen.

~ Night 6 ~

THIS DAY IS DONE

Oh, good and gracious and loving Father, how I love knowing this day is done and You are with me as I prepare for rest. How grateful I am that You walked through the moments of today with me, guiding me and fighting for me in ways I do not even know about. Thank You for bringing me safely through the day. Thank You for all of the ways You provided for me. And Thank You for the glimpses of You I saw in the world today (feel free to name specific ways God revealed Himself to you today).

Tonight, God, as I wind down and prepare for sleep, let my thoughts be on You. Let my mind be filled with snippets of conversation I wish to share with You and not on worries or anxieties. Remind me in this very moment that You have all of my cares in Your hands. In fact, You have me in Your hands. Let my every breath be a whisper of gratitude and worship as I drift into sleep. Grant me rest and restore my soul tonight. I love knowing that You never sleep and are always watching over me and because of this truth, because You are the same yesterday, today, and forever, I know I am safe here, watched over by You. Thank You for being the refuge I need and for inviting me to rest deeply tonight.

In Jesus' name I pray, Amen.

~ Night 7 ~

I SLEEP IN PEACE

Dear Lord, my gracious heavenly Father, I come into Your presence tonight and give You thanks for who You are and for Your faithfulness. I thank You for Your promises and for Your presence. I thank You for Your unconditional, no-matter-what, abounding love and abundant grace. As I prepare for sleep tonight, I consider the words of David: "I will both lie down and sleep in peace, for you alone, LORD, make me live in safety" (Psalm 4:8 CSB), and I give You thanks for the peace You pour over me so that I can rest well tonight because I rest in the shadow of Your protecting presence. You are always with me and You watch over me and I am deeply grateful.

God, sometimes the days are long and they bring difficulties and challenges that feel overwhelming. Even so, You are with me as You were with David, and that is why I recall his words that even when he felt as though he were walking through the darkest shadows of death and devastation, he knew You were with him. Like David, I pour out my heart and give You my thanks as this day comes to its end. Thank You for sustaining me by Your mighty right hand. Be with me also tonight and give me rest so that I am restored in You.

I pray this in Jesus' name, Amen.

Also by Judith Heaney

A forty day Lenten journey that places you in the middle of Jesus' journey to the cross. Experience Lent and the extravagant love of Jesus in a new way as you immerse yourself in the presence of the Savior. This journey with Jesus will reignite your intimacy with Christ by drawing you into the story of His suffering, crucifixion, and resurrection alongside His disciples.

www.ingramcontent.com/pod-product-compliance
Lightning Source LLC
Chambersburg PA
CBHW072009290426
44109CB00018B/2183